HO
SCIE

by
Briant Smith

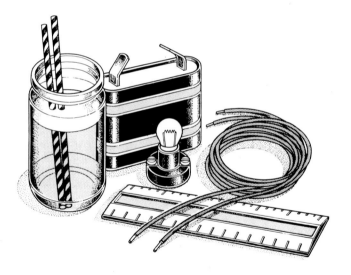

Piccolo
A Piper Book

Contents

Introduction   **4**
The scientific method

1: Kitchen Chemicals   **6**
Using an indicator; Homemade indicators;
Testing for strength; The washing soda test

2: Science and Food   **12**
The iodine test; The spit and starch test;
Fatty foods; Keeping us clean; Cooking
chemistry; Baking bread

3: Ink Experiments   **18**
Separating the dyes in ink

4: Energy and Ourselves   **20**
Measuring work; Supplying the muscles

5: Energy at Home   **23**
Making electrical circuits; What do fuses do?;
Build a quiz board; Copper plating a key;
Electricity and magnetism; Making an
electromagnet; Make an electric bell

6: Electronics   **34**
Resistors; Using a transistor; Light
dependent resistors; Building the 'magic candle'

7: Mirrors and Lenses   **39**
Make your own periscope; Bending light;
Making a telescope

8: Keeping warm   **42**
Investigating convection; Which materials
conduct heat?; Keeping heat in

9: An All-Purpose Liquid   **45**
What dissolves in water?; Why do we need
water?; Floating and sinking; Salt water and
fresh water; Why does a ship float?; How
much can a boat carry?; Finding the right shape;
Making a submarine; A design problem

10: On the Surface   **54**
Floating a needle; Altering surface tension;
The cotton loop trick; A mothball-powered boat;
Insects and surface tension

11: What is Soil?   **58**
How much water does soil contain?; Will soil
burn?; Separating the soil 'skeleton';
Measuring the air in soil; Is your garden acid
or alkaline?; Why use fertilizers?; Comparing
soils; What minerals must soil have?; Living
things in the soil

12: Looking at Plants   **70**
Making a leaf collection; Fruits and seeds;
How far can seeds fly?; What do plant stems do?

Glossary   **76**
Index   **78**
Acknowledgements   **80**

Introduction

Over the centuries, scientific discoveries have led to the development of many of the marvels of the world today – from electrical appliances and modern medicine to motor cars and space rockets. Scientists are people who ask questions and then try to find the answers to those questions. One of the most important ways of doing this is by setting up experiments and recording the results.

In this book, you will find experiments that will help you to look at very ordinary things in a new way. They will help you to discover a number of important things, such as what foods are made of, how electrical circuits work, why things float and how soil helps plants grow. Above all, they will help you to understand what science is all about.

The scientific method

Remember that scientists need to work carefully and accurately. Do not worry if an experiment does not work well the first time. Just check through the instructions carefully and try again. If you find you have real problems, ask an adult to help you.

Watch your experiments carefully and keep a record of your results. As you work on your experiments ask yourself questions. Why does it happen? How does it happen? The answers will help you to understand how things work.

Ask the same questions about other things that you see happening around you. Try to think of ways of finding out the answers. You will probably think of many experiments to do that are not mentioned in this book. This process of looking at things, having ideas and testing them by experiments is how all science works.

Finally, a word of warning. Experiments are fun to do, but they can also be dangerous. WHEREVER SAFETY INSTRUCTIONS ARE GIVEN, TAKE SPECIAL CARE TO OBSERVE THEM. If you think up other experiments of your own, check them with an adult first to be sure they are safe. BE PARTICULARLY CAREFUL WHEN DEALING WITH CHEMICALS AND NAKED FLAMES, AND NEVER EXPERIMENT WITH MAINS ELECTRICITY UNDER ANY CIRCUMSTANCES.

1: Kitchen Chemicals

Everything around us is made of chemicals, and some of the most important chemicals in the house are found in the kitchen. All food consists of chemicals, and so do other kitchen items, such as household cleaners and disinfectants.

In science, it may be important to know if a chemical belongs to either one of two groups – **acids** or **alkalis**. An acid is a substance that tastes sour, such as the juice of a lemon. There are hundreds of different kinds of acids. Some, like lemon juice, are weak and harmless. But strong acids, like the sulphuric acid found in car batteries, are very harmful and must not even be allowed to touch your skin. So NEVER test for acids by tasting them.

Alkalis can also be weak and harmless or strong and harmful. They are the chemical opposites of acids. An alkali is simply a substance that reduces the *acidity* of an acid when mixed with it. Milk of magnesia, for example, helps to relieve indigestion by reducing the acidity in a person's stomach.

The safest and simplest way of finding out if a substance is an acid or an alkali is by using a

chemical called an **indicator**. When an indicator is mixed with any other chemical it changes colour. By comparing the colour of the mixture with the colours on a special chart, the chemical can be given a **pH value**.

On pages 8–9 you will find a colour chart for an indicator known as 'Universal Indicator'.

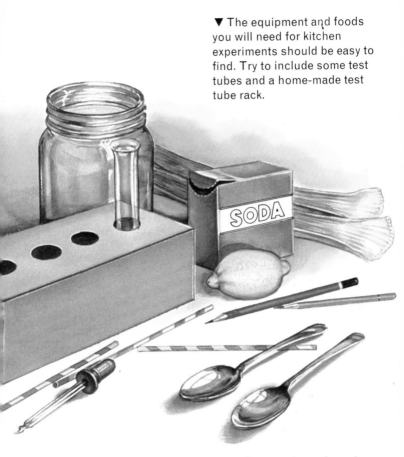

▼ The equipment and foods you will need for kitchen experiments should be easy to find. Try to include some test tubes and a home-made test tube rack.

From this you can see that a strong acid has a pH value of 1, a **neutral** (neither acid nor alkaline) substance has a pH value of 7, and a strong alkali has a pH value of 14.

Using an indicator

Indicator **solution** can be bought as part of a simple soil test kit (see page 63). Look around several garden shops and ironmongers to find a cheap one. Small test tubes should be provided in the kit, but a few larger ones are useful and can be found in most major toy shops. Make a simple rack for your test tubes by cutting holes in a small wooden or cardboard box, as shown in the drawing above.

pH	1	2	3	4	5	6
Colour						

Acid

Put about 1 cm depth of water in a test tube and add ten drops of the indicator solution using the dropper provided in the kit. Look at the colour chart from your kit and write down the pH value of the water (NOTE: some tap water is slightly acid).

Now repeat the test using lemon juice, vinegar and the juice from rhubarb. Are these foods acid or alkaline? Make solutions of things like bicarbonate of soda or washing soda by adding a very small amount to some water. Then test these solutions with the indicator. Because some substances contain dyes you may get colours slightly different to the ones shown on your chart.

Homemade indicators
You can also make your own indicators from some plants.

INDICATOR	Colour with vinegar	Colour with water	Colour with washing soda
Cabbage juice			
Beetroot juice			

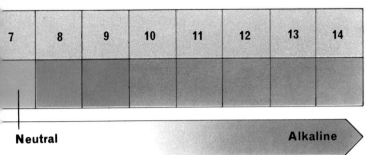

7	8	9	10	11	12	13	14

Neutral   **Alkaline**

▲ A colour chart for Universal Indicator.

One of the best is red cabbage. Take a few leaves and cut them up into small pieces on a chopping board. Put the pieces in a saucepan and just cover them with water. Bring the water to the boil and let it simmer for 15 minutes. Check the water level at intervals, so that it does not boil dry.

Allow the liquid to cool and then filter it through wet blotting paper, buttermuslin or an old handkerchief. You can make a funnel from the top of an old washing-up liquid container turned upside down. Throw out the leaves and keep the filtered cabbage water. This is your indicator solution.

To find the neutral colour of your indicator, mix a few drops with water. Then mix a few drops with vinegar to find the colour when acid. Do the same with washing soda to find the colour when alkaline. Make a copy of the chart shown on the opposite page and write in the colours that you see.

Simmer chopped cabbage for 15 minutes

Filter cool cabbage water into a bottle

9

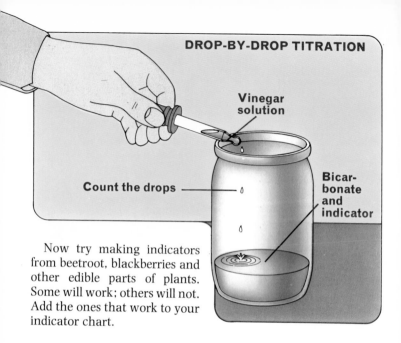

DROP-BY-DROP TITRATION

Vinegar solution

Count the drops

Bicarbonate and indicator

Now try making indicators from beetroot, blackberries and other edible parts of plants. Some will work; others will not. Add the ones that work to your indicator chart.

Testing for strength
The strength of an alkali can be tested by mixing it with an indicator and then adding an acid until a colour change is seen. (Testing an acid for strength works in the same way, but the mixtures are reversed.) This process is used in laboratories and is called **titration.** You can do a simple titration experiment using an eye dropper (which you can buy from a chemist) and a few small jars.

You will need two 'stock' solutions. Make up a stock alkali solution by dissolving a level teaspoonful of bicarbonate of soda in a teacupful of warm water. Similarly, make up a stock acid by adding a teaspoonful of vinegar to a teacupful of water.

For your first titration put five droppers full of bicarbonate solution into a clean jar and then add ten drops of indicator (from the soil test kit). Wash out the eye dropper carefully and fill it with vinegar solution. Add this, drop by drop, to the bicarbonate/indicator solution in the jar, as shown above. Count the number of drops as they fall, and gently shake the jar occasionally to mix the solutions. Stop when the colour changes to green. This is known as the *end point*, which is reached when you have a neutral solution in the jar. Write down the number of drops you needed to reach the end point. This will give you a figure for the strength of your bicarbonate (alkaline) solution.

To be sure that your results are accurate, you should repeat this titration at least four times. Now try the same experiment with your homemade indicators. Some will give good end points (that is, good, sharp colour changes), and others will not.

You can also try testing different acids against your stock alkali (bicarbonate) solution, and different alkalis against your stock acid (vinegar) solution. For each new acid or alkali you test it is best to do a quick trial run first. If an acid/alkali is very strong you may get no end point at all, in which case you will need to dilute it with water and try again. BE CAREFUL WHICH HOUSEHOLD CHEMICALS YOU CHOOSE, AS SOME CAN BE HARMFUL TO YOUR SKIN. If you are in doubt check with an adult first.

The washing soda test

For this experiment it is best to use Universal Indicator. Try asking your science teacher for some. Otherwise, use the soil test indicator.

The main stages are shown in the drawings above. First, fill a jam jar until it is three-quarters full with water. Add two droppers full of vinegar and half a dropper of indicator (1). Drop in a few lumps of washing soda (2) and leave the jar where it will not get moved (3). Watch what happens to the solution over the next few days.

2: Science and Food

We eat food because we like it, or because we get hungry. We get hungry because our bodies need regular amounts of certain chemicals in order to stay healthy. Food contains many chemicals, the most important of these being carbohydrates, fats, proteins, vitamins and minerals.

Not all foods contain the same chemicals, however. If they did, we could all live on, say, baked beans and not bother to eat anything else! So it is important to know which chemicals are found in which foods and what happens when they are cooked and eaten.

The iodine test

There are different types of **carbohydrates** in foods, but all of them give our bodies energy. Starch is one important carbohydrate found in many foods. The test for starch is simple. You will need some iodine (from a chemist) and an eye dropper.

Put a few drops of iodine onto a piece of food. If the food contains starch, the iodine will turn from brown to a blue-black colour. Make up a chart like the one shown below and test a number of different foods. Cut vegetables like potatoes and beans in half and test the inside.

Food	Starch	No Starch
Potato	✓	
Bread	✓	
Salt		✗
Baked Beans		
Runner Beans		
Cabbage		

The spit and starch test

In order for our bodies to make use of the food we eat, the chemicals in the food have to be broken down. This process is called **digestion.** The actual job of breaking down the food is done by special chemicals called **enzymes.**

Digestion starts in the mouth. As you chew food, it mixes with your saliva (spit), which contains an enzyme. Slowly chew a piece of bread and see what changes you notice in the feel and taste of the bread.

Now try the following experiment to see how the enzyme in your saliva affects starch. First, rinse out your mouth with water. Chew a clean rubber band to make some saliva, then wash out your mouth with an eggcupful of water and spit this into a small jar. Label this jar 'spit solution'.

Make a 'starch solution' by adding a quarter of a teaspoonful of flour to a larger jar full of water.

Stir the starch solution and then take an eggcupful and mix it with your spit solution. After two minutes remove a sample of the mixture, using a straw. Gently push the straw to the bottom of the jar and place your thumb over the top end of it (**1**). This will trap some of the mixture so that you can lift it onto a white plastic lid. Lift your thumb to release the liquid. Now add a drop of iodine to the

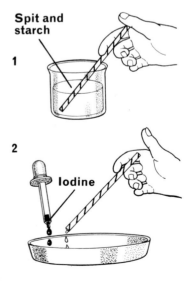

Spit and starch

1

Iodine

2

THE GREASE SPOT TEST

MILK	BUTTER	WATER	COOKING OIL
VINEGAR	CABBAGE WATER	MARGARINE	POTATO

sample and see if it changes colour (2).

Repeat the test at two-minute intervals, using a fresh sample and a clean lid each time. When the iodine no longer changes colour the enzyme in your spit solution will have completely broken down the starch. Keep a record of how many samples you test before this happens, so that you know how long it takes for the enzyme to work.

You can test your friends' spit in the same way, to compare their saliva with your own. Remember to stir the starch solution each time.

Fatty foods
Like carbohydrates, **fats** give us energy. A quick way of testing for fats is to rub a piece of food

(or its juice) onto a piece of plain paper. Leave the paper to dry and then hold it up to the light. If the food contains fat, the paper will show a greasy spot that lets light through. The drawing above shows the sort of results you would get with some foods. Try testing other foods in the same way.

Keeping us clean
Finding out about food chemicals has other uses as well as keeping us healthy. You often see advertisements for 'biological' washing powders, for example. But why are these washing powders different from any others?

The reason is that biological washing powders have had enzymes added to them. These enzymes dissolve away **protein** stains on clothes by 'digesting' them, in much the same way as our body enzymes digest the proteins that we eat. You can test this by a simple experiment.

Cut some cloth into nine small pieces and smear some egg yolk onto each one. You could also add smears of blood from a piece of uncooked meat, if you wish. Let the stains dry. Put each piece of cloth into a jar and split the jars up into three groups of three. Label one jar in each group 'Cold', one 'Warm' and one 'Hot'.

Put a little ordinary washing powder into the jars in one group, and some biological washing powder into another group. Then add cold, warm or hot water to all three groups according to the labels. Gently shake the jars (take care with the hot ones!) and then look at the pieces of cloth every five minutes. Which jar gives the best results?

Cooking chemistry

Because foods contain chemicals, cooking food is also a form of chemistry. So it can help to know what happens to ingredients when they are mixed and heated.

One example of this is the use of yeast in some foods. Yeast is a fungus that is used in making wine, beer and baking bread.

1. **Water only**

2. **Water and ordinary washing powder**

3. **Water and biological washing powder**

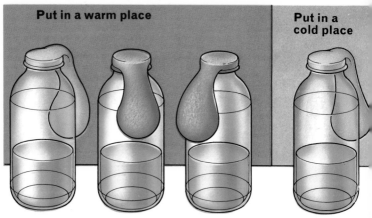

Put in a warm place

Put in a cold place

Yeast and water

Sugar and water

Yeast, sugar and water

Yeast, sugar and water

Yeast feeds on sugar and produces alcohol and carbon dioxide gas. You can test part of this effect with the following experiment.

You will need four balloons that will fit over the necks of four bottles, some baker's yeast (from most food shops) and some sugar. Half fill each bottle with water and add a teaspoonful of yeast or sugar, or both, as indicated in the drawing above. Label the bottles to show what they contain and firmly attach a balloon to the top of each one. Leave three bottles (as shown) in a warm place and one in a cold place, for about two days.

What happens to the balloons? Does the same thing happen in each bottle? If not, why do you think this is so?

Baking bread

Collect together the following ingredients:

450 grammes (1 lb) plain flour
1 teaspoonful salt
20 grammes ($\frac{1}{2}$ oz) yeast
$\frac{1}{4}$ teaspoonful sugar
300 ml ($\frac{1}{2}$ pint) warm water
a small amount of lard

Sift the flour and mix it with the salt in a warm bowl. Mix the yeast and sugar together in a jug and then mix in the warm water.

Make a 'well' in the middle of the flour and pour in the yeast mixture. Mix the flour from the centre of the bowl until you have a thick batter (**1**). Sprinkle some of the remaining flour from the edge on top of the batter and cover the bowl with a damp cloth. Leave it in a warm place for 15 to 20 minutes. When bubbles have started to show on the surface, work in the rest of the flour and then tip the dough onto a floured table or board. Knead the dough until it is no longer sticky (2). Put it into a clean, warm bowl that has been lightly greased with lard. Cover the bowl with a cloth or polythene bag (3) and leave it to stand in a warm place (70–80°F / 20–28°C) for 1 to 1½ hours until the dough is twice its original size.

Remove the dough and knead it lightly. Shape it and put it into a warm, lightly greased baking tin. Leave this in a warm place for about 15 minutes, then put the tin into a preheated oven at 400°F/180°C (mark 6) for 35 to 40 mins. (4). Why do you think yeast is used in making bread? What does it do?

MAKING BREAD

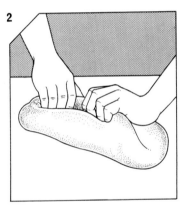

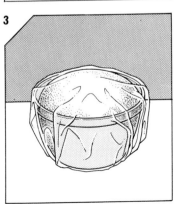

3: Ink Experiments

In science laboratories it is often necessary to separate two chemicals, or to find out how many chemicals a particular substance consists of. One way of doing this is to use a process called 'chromatography'.

push this through the centre of the square. Then soak the top of the wick with ink from a black felt-tip pen.

Half fill the jar with water and place the paper on top of the jar as shown. Watch what

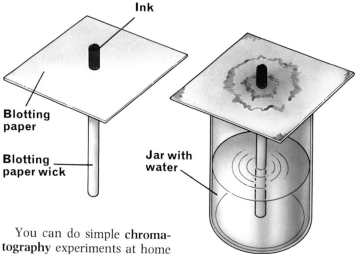

Ink

Blotting paper

Blotting paper wick

Jar with water

You can do simple **chromatography** experiments at home to find out which colours are present in inks, dyes and food colourings.

Separating the dyes in ink
Cut out a square of white blotting paper big enough to fit over a jar. Roll up another piece of blotting paper to act as a wick, as shown above, and

happens over about twenty minutes, as the water climbs the wick and spreads out over the flat piece of blotting paper.

You can test a variety of inks, felt tips and dyes by this method, but it is rather slow. To test several inks at the same time, fold a piece of blotting

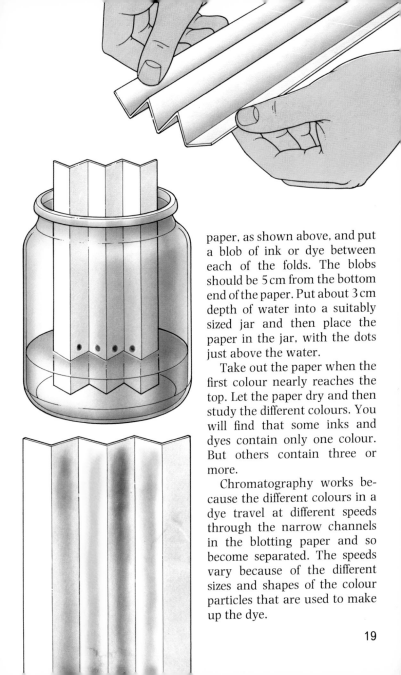

paper, as shown above, and put a blob of ink or dye between each of the folds. The blobs should be 5 cm from the bottom end of the paper. Put about 3 cm depth of water into a suitably sized jar and then place the paper in the jar, with the dots just above the water.

Take out the paper when the first colour nearly reaches the top. Let the paper dry and then study the different colours. You will find that some inks and dyes contain only one colour. But others contain three or more.

Chromatography works because the different colours in a dye travel at different speeds through the narrow channels in the blotting paper and so become separated. The speeds vary because of the different sizes and shapes of the colour particles that are used to make up the dye.

4: Energy and Ourselves

Food provides us with the energy we need for all the different processes that go on inside our bodies. But most of our energy is used in processes that involve movement, such as lifting an arm or a leg. Using energy in this way means that we are doing 'work'. In scientific terms, doing 'work' means that we are using a 'force' to make something move. Most of the force we use is needed to overcome gravity, which is the force that holds us on the ground.

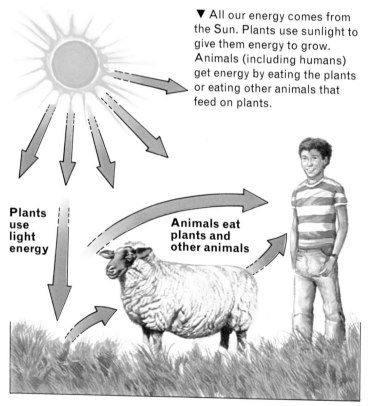

▼ All our energy comes from the Sun. Plants use sunlight to give them energy to grow. Animals (including humans) get energy by eating the plants or eating other animals that feed on plants.

Plants use light energy

Animals eat plants and other animals

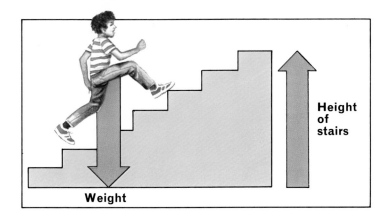

Height of stairs

Weight

The amount of force used to move something is measured in units called *newtons*. The amount of **work** you do (and the energy you use) to produce this force is measured in *joules.*

Measuring work

To find out how many joules (how much work) it takes for you to overcome gravity and run up a flight of stairs, for example, you have to multiply the force used (in newtons) by the vertical distance moved (in metres). Try doing this calculation yourself.

First, you have to find out the amount of force (newtons) you use to move your body to the top of the stairs. To do this you simply multiply your weight (in kilogrammes) by 10.

Next, you need to know the vertical distance (the height) of the staircase. A quick way of doing this is to measure the height of one step and multiply this by the total number of steps.

If your weight is 30 kilogrammes and the height of the stairs is 3 metres, the calculation is as follows:
Force is $30 \times 10 = 300$ newtons. Height is 3 metres. Therefore, work done is $300 \times 3 = 900$ joules.

Measuring power

You can also calculate your **power** – the *rate* at which you do work. Ask a friend to time how fast you can run up the stairs. To be very accurate you will need a stopwatch.

Power is measured in *watts.* To calculate your power you divide the work done (e.g. 900 joules) by the time taken (in seconds). If your power is 373 watts, you are rated at $\frac{1}{2}$ horsepower (1 horsepower = 746 watts). Can you beat this?

Supplying the muscles

When you do work, your breathing rate and pulse rate both increase to supply extra energy to your muscles. You can feel your pulse rate by placing the two middle fingers of one hand on the inside of your wrist, below the fleshy base of your thumb. Count the number of beats in a minute. Then count the number of breaths you take in a minute.

Now take some sort of violent exercise, such as running on the spot, for several minutes. Then count your breathing rate again and get a friend to count your pulse rate at the same time, for each minute until they both return to normal. Write down the results as you count, and plot some graphs to show the results. How does your recovery compare with the graphs shown here?

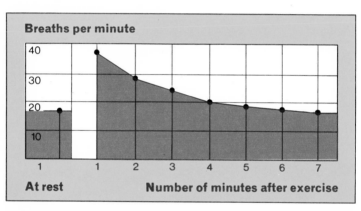

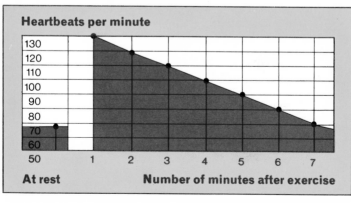

5: Energy at Home

Energy can take a number of different forms. The energy we use in our bodies is the chemical energy stored in food. Other kinds of energy are mechanical energy, heat, light and electrical energy.

Energy can be changed from one form into another. Electrical energy, for example, is converted into heat and light in our homes. And most of the electricity we use is produced by converting heat energy, made by burning fossil fuels such as coal and oil, into electrical energy.

Fossil fuels are formed from the remains of plants and animals that once used energy from the Sun. So, like the chemical energy in food, most

▲ Electricity is produced at power stations (above). Transformers deliver high-voltage electricity along thick cables. Before electricity reaches our homes (below) the voltage is reduced by other transformers (a small one can be seen attached to the telegraph pole).

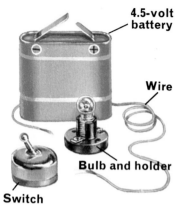

4.5-volt battery

Wire

Bulb and holder

Switch

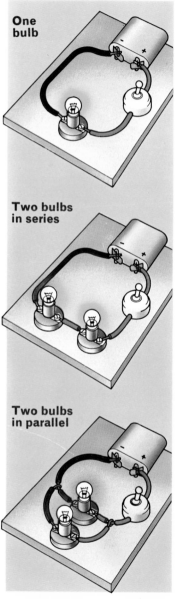

One bulb

Two bulbs in series

Two bulbs in parallel

forms of energy originate from the Sun.

Making electrical circuits

Much of the energy supplied to your home is likely to be in the form of electrical energy. This type of electricity is known as *mains electricity*, which is very powerful. YOU MUST NEVER ATTEMPT TO DO ANY EXPERIMENTS USING MAINS ELECTRICITY. It is very dangerous and could even kill you!

You can, however, find out some of the ways in which electricity is used in your home by building simple electrical **circuits** powered by batteries.

For these experiments you will need some small bulbholders (at least two) and bulbs, a few small switches, a 4.5-volt and a 6-volt battery and two or three metres of low voltage wire (0.1 mm). These can all be

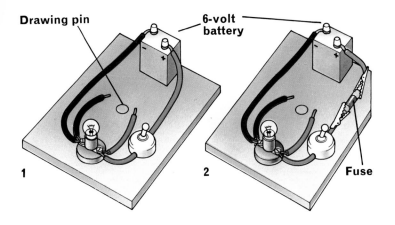

Drawing pin

6-volt battery

1

2   **Fuse**

bought from most large toy and model shops and from some electrical shops. You will also need some crocodile clips and a 1-amp fuse. These can be bought from a car accessory shop. Finally, a flat piece of wood to build circuits on is also useful.

Connect up the simple circuit shown in the top drawing on page 24. Carefully cut away the plastic insulation from around the ends of the wires. You can connect the wires to the 4.5-volt battery by using paper clips as shown. The switch and bulbholder have screws for holding the wires. The bulb should now light up when the switch is turned on.

Next, make up the circuits shown in the two lower drawings, with two bulbs in series and two bulbs in parallel. If you do not have enough

batteries and bulbs to build both circuits at the same time, build one first and then the other. What happens in each case when you switch on? Which system do you think would be the best for wiring up two lights in a room?

What do fuses do?
Every electrical circuit in your house has its own fuse and so do the plugs of most appliances. These are put in to break the circuit if something goes wrong.

Wire up the first circuit again, but this time use the 6-volt battery and connect an extra piece of wire to each of the screws on the bulbholder, as in the first drawing above. Switch on to make sure the circuit is working properly. Switch off again and connect the bare ends of the extra wires

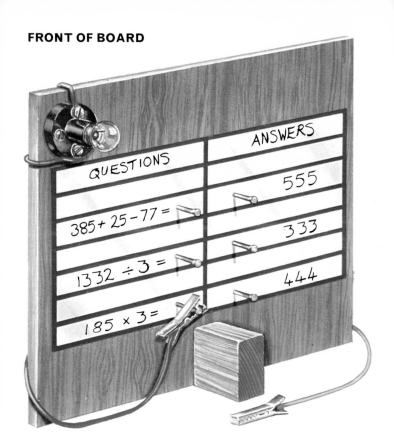

to a drawing pin. This makes what is called a 'short circuit'. Switch on again. Does the bulb light up? What happens to the wires in the circuit if you leave the switch on for about a minute? Switch off and carefully feel the wire. Can you imagine what would happen if the mains electricity in your house was short-circuited in this way?

Now look at the second drawing on page 25, and add two crocodile clips and a 1-amp fuse to the circuit. Test the circuit with the bare ends disconnected. Then reconnect the loose ends and switch on again. What happens this time?

Now remove the fuse and replace it with one fine strand of wire taken from a short length (about 5 cm) of 0.1 mm wire.

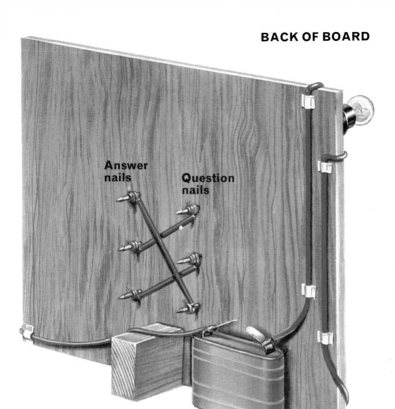

BACK OF BOARD

Answer nails

Question nails

Again, switch on and see what happens.

Build a quiz board

You will need a piece of 6-mm thick plywood (about 20 cm × 25 cm). Draw some lines on a piece of white card and pin or glue it to one side of the board, as shown opposite. Carefully hammer in six 25-mm (1-inch) nails in the

positions shown, so that the heads and tips stick out on each side of the board. Glue a small wooden block onto each side, so that the board will stand up by itself.

Fix a small bulb and holder to the top corner of the board and wire up a 4.5-volt battery to the bulbholder and two crocodile clips as shown. Touch the crocodile clips together to make sure that the bulb lights up. Finally, join up the nails at the back of the board with short pieces of 0.1-mm wire. Connect each 'question nail' to a different 'answer nail', wrapping the bare ends of the wires tightly round the nails.

The questions and answers can be anything you choose, such as simple mathematical problems and their solutions, or the names of countries and their capitals. Put the questions in the three spaces on the left of the board. Jumble up the answers on the opposite side, but arrange them so that when the crocodile clips are attached to the correct question and answer nails, the bulb lights up.

Now try the questions on your friends and see if they can get the right answers. You can think up more questions and answers, too. But remember to change the connections at the back of the board so that the positions of the correct answers are not always the same.

Copper plating a key

Electricity has many uses. It can be used not only to provide heating and lighting but also to alter chemicals. For example, it is used in a process known as **electroplating**, in which one type of metal is coated with a thin layer of another metal.

For this experiment you will need some copper sulphate.

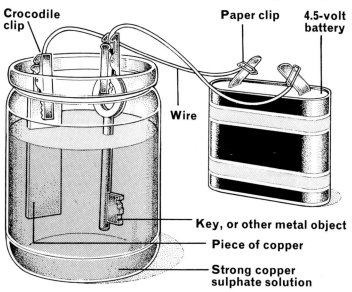

Crocodile clip

Paper clip

4.5-volt battery

Wire

Key, or other metal object

Piece of copper

Strong copper sulphate solution

Some garden shops will have it, or try larger toy shops that keep chemistry sets. You will also need a piece of clean copper (a bit of copper pipe will do) and two other metal objects, such as keys.

Dissolve as much copper sulphate as you can in a jar of water. Using one of the keys, wire up the circuit as shown in the drawing below left. Connect the key to the negative terminal of the battery and make sure it is not touching the piece of copper. What happens to the key after a few minutes?

Now remove the key and replace it with the second one. But this time, also include a bulb and holder in the circuit, between the key and the battery (you may need to use longer pieces of wire). Again, watch what happens to the key.

In both cases, you will see that the electric current from the battery causes copper to be deposited on the key. At the same time, copper is being removed from the piece of copper. (NOTE: This process will stop after a few minutes, so to complete the second key you may have to ask an adult to add a few drops of sulphuric acid from a car battery to the copper sulphate solution. This will restart the process. BE CARE-FUL, SULPHURIC ACID BURNS SKIN AND CLOTHING.)

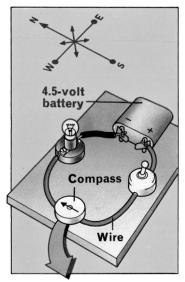

▲ Detecting the magnetic effect of an electric current. Place the compass on the wire and turn the board so that the needle points along the wire.

When you have plated both keys, compare the results. Now see if you can clean the keys. Try the circuit with a plated key connected to the positive ter-minal of the battery.

Electricity and magnetism
Another effect of electricity is that it produces magnetism. When an electric current flows through a wire an invisible magnetic field is created around the wire. This can be de-monstrated by using the circuit shown in the drawing above.

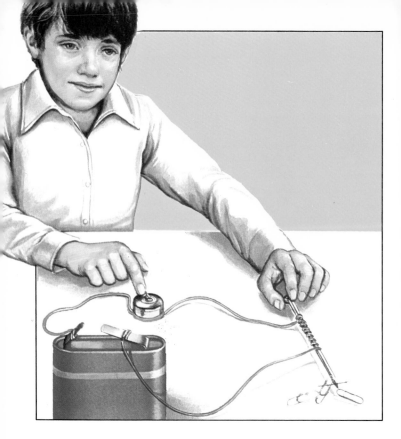

You will need a small, cheap compass. Make sure that the compass needle is in line with the wire underneath the compass. Turn on the switch and see what happens to the needle.

Now try the experiment again, but this time leave the bulb and holder out of the circuit and only switch on for a few seconds. What difference do you think the bulb makes to the strength of the magnetic field?

▲ A simple electromagnet can be made by winding some wire round an iron or steel nail. Connect one end of the wire to a switch and the other to a 4.5-volt battery. Connect up the battery to the switch and switch on.

In both experiments you will see the compass needle move. This shows that there is a change in the magnetic field around the wire and that this change must be due to the flow of the electric current.

The relationship between electricity and magnetism also works the other way round. Magnetism can be used to create an electric current. An electricity generator at a power station has a huge magnet that spins inside a giant coil of wire. As the magnet turns, the magnetic field moves through the wire in the coil and causes an electric current to flow along it. The magnet is often turned by steam power, which is created by burning fossil fuels.

Making an electromagnet

You can use the magnetic effect of an electric current to make yourself a temporary magnet as shown in the drawing opposite. This type of magnet is called, not surprisingly, an **electromagnet.** It works by using the magnetic field produced by an electric current to make a piece of iron become temporarily magnetized. The magnet can be switched on and off simply by switching the current on and off.

Your electromagnet will pick up objects such as pins and paper clips. What other materials will it pick up? Draw up a chart to record which objects respond to magnetism and which do not.

Make an electric bell

An electric bell uses an electro-magnet to make and break an electrical circuit. As it does so, the bell's clapper strikes the gong repeatedly.

You can make your own electric bell, but you will need some help from an adult. You will need a wooden base-board (about 20 cm × 30 cm), a tin can (for the gong), some nuts, bolts and screws of various sizes, two strips of *springy* steel (about 15 cm and 8 cm long) and three small blocks of wood. You may find all these things lying around at home, or see if your local ironmonger or garage can help. You will also need a 4.5-volt battery, a push switch and about a metre of enamelled copper wire. Go to an electrical shop for these.

Look carefully at the draw-ings on the next two pages. First, glue one block of wood to the base-board, about 10 cm from one end (**a**). Ask an adult to drill and shape the strips of steel for you, so that you can bolt them together and screw the larger one (the clapper strip) to the wooden block. Fix a small nut and bolt through a hole at the free end of the clapper.

Get a hole drilled in the second wooden block, large enough to push your largest bolt through it (**b**). Wind some of the enamelled wire round

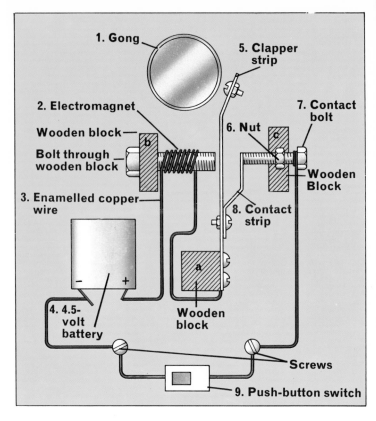

1. Gong
5. Clapper strip
2. Electromagnet
7. Contact bolt
6. Nut
Wooden block
Bolt through wooden block
Wooden Block
3. Enamelled copper wire
8. Contact strip
4. 4.5-volt battery
Wooden block
Screws
9. Push-button switch

this bolt to make the electromagnet. Position the electromagnet a centimetre or so from the steel clapper strip. Now scrape the enamel from the ends of the electromagnet wire and just touch the bare ends (FOR A FEW SECONDS ONLY) to the battery terminals to see if the electromagnet will pull the strip towards it. When you have found the best place for the electromagnet, glue the wooden block firmly to the base-board.

Now get a hole drilled in the bottom of the tin can and screw it in place, so that the clapper strikes it when the magnet attracts the steel strip.

A second, smaller bolt must now be fixed so that the smaller steel strip (the contact strip) touches it when the bell is switched off. Glue the third wooden block to the base-

AN ELECTRIC BELL

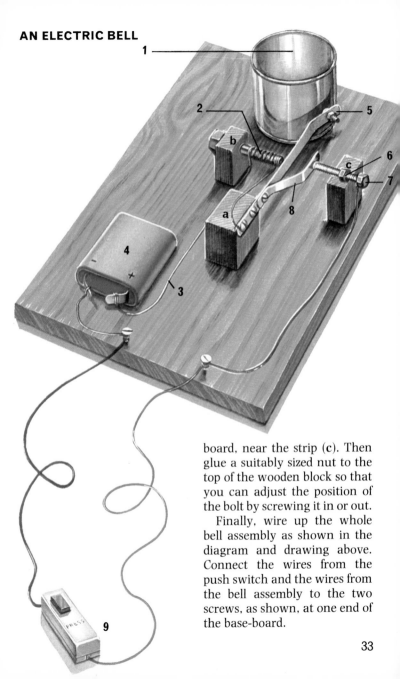

board, near the strip (**c**). Then glue a suitably sized nut to the top of the wooden block so that you can adjust the position of the bolt by screwing it in or out.

Finally, wire up the whole bell assembly as shown in the diagram and drawing above. Connect the wires from the push switch and the wires from the bell assembly to the two screws, as shown, at one end of the base-board.

6: Electronics

In the last forty years, our lives have been greatly changed by new types of electrical devices that use electronic components, such as transistors. Simple electronic devices are quite easy to make and great fun to use. The 'magic candle' described in this chapter will amaze your friends as you 'light' the bulb with a taper and then appear to 'blow' it out.

For your 'candle' you will need the two **resistors** shown on this page, a BC 108 **transistor** (shown on the opposite page), a **light dependent resistor** (see page 36), and a 0.06-amp bulb. You may be able to buy all these at your local electrical repair shop. If not, try a model making shop. If you have difficulty in your area, write to a supplier of electronic apparatus. An address is given on page 80.

You will also need a bulb-holder, some 0.1-mm wire and a 6-volt battery (see NOTE on page 36).

Resistors

Successful electronics depends on being able to control the flow of current in a circuit. Resistors, as their name suggests, control current by 'resisting' its flow

RESISTORS

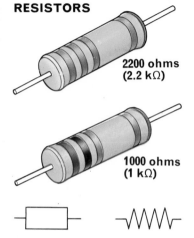

2200 ohms
(2.2 kΩ)

1000 ohms
(1 kΩ)

Symbols used in circuit diagrams

through a circuit. A resistor looks like a small cylinder with a wire at each end. The bands of colour on the outside are a code for the value of its resistance, which is measured in ohms (Ω).

The two resistors in the magic candle are used to cause different amounts of current to flow in different parts of the circuit.

Using a transistor

Transistors play an important part in many electronic devices. They are often used as electrically-controlled switches, and in the magic candle a transistor is used to switch the current to the bulb on and off.

Transistors are easily damaged, so treat yours with care. IT IS VITAL to use a low current (0.06-amp) bulb in a circuit that contains a transistor, otherwise the transistor will overheat and be ruined.

A transistor has three wires, or legs, known as the *emitter*, the *collector* and the *base*. Take care not to break off these legs and make sure that you wire them up correctly. Look for a small tag or paint spot near one of the legs. This tells you which is the emitter leg. Always wire up the EMITTER leg to the NEGATIVE terminal of the battery.

The easiest way to connect up a transistor is to use plastic sheathing, as shown in the diagram on the right (use small-bore earth sheathing from an electrical shop). Alternatively, get an adult to help you solder the connections. But take care not to overheat the transistor. Holding each leg with a small pair of pliers helps to take away the heat before it can do any damage.

Light dependent resistors

Not all resistors have fixed resistances. A light dependent resistor, or LDR, varies in resistance according to the

TRANSISTOR

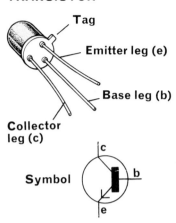

Tag

Emitter leg (e)

Base leg (b)

Collector leg (c)

Symbol

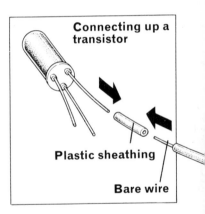

Connecting up a transistor

Plastic sheathing

Bare wire

amount of light that falls on it. In the dark, an LDR has a very high resistance and so prevents current from flowing in a circuit. In the light, however, the resistance is much lower, allowing a current to flow.

Wire up the circuit shown in the diagram on the next page. This type of diagram is called a

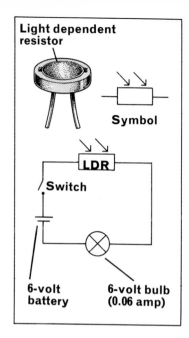

Light dependent resistor

Symbol

LDR

Switch

6-volt battery

6-volt bulb (0.06 amp)

orange squash or fabric softener container.

Cut the container up, as shown in the diagram below (you may need some help with this). Thread two wires through the handle and connect the LDR to the top of these wires with plastic sheathing (or by soldering). Position the LDR just inside the top of the handle and use plasticine to hold it in place.

Wire up all the components, carefully following the circuit diagram on the right. The wires do not have to be coloured as shown, but colours do help to avoid confusion. (NOTE: A single 6-volt battery may be too big for your container. If it is, buy four 1.5-volt pencil light

circuit diagram. It uses symbols to show you the components you need and their position in a circuit. Make the connections to the LDR using plastic sheathing, as you will want the LDR again.

Cover the LDR with your hand and switch on. Does the bulb light up? Now slowly move your hand away from the LDR. What happens?

Building the 'magic candle'
To make the holder for your candle, you will need a cardboard tube, some pieces of flat cardboard and a large, empty plastic container, such as an

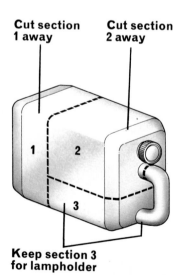

Cut section 1 away   **Cut section 2 away**

1   2

3

Keep section 3 for lampholder

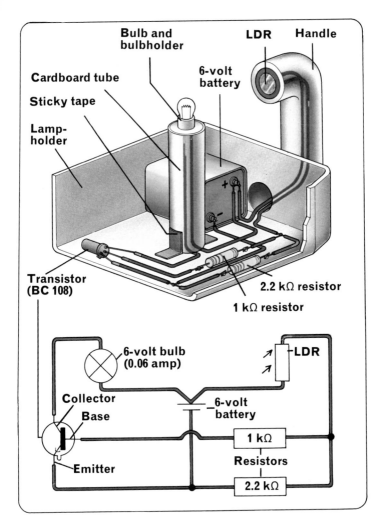

Bulb and bulbholder

LDR

Handle

Cardboard tube

6-volt battery

Sticky tape

Lamp-holder

Transistor (BC 108)

2.2 kΩ resistor

1 kΩ resistor

6-volt bulb (0.06 amp)

LDR

Collector

Base

6-volt battery

1 kΩ

Resistors

Emitter

2.2 kΩ

batteries with a special holder and connectors from an electrical shop. Correctly arranged – wired end to end in series – these batteries will give you 6 volts.)

Mount the bulbholder and bulb at the top of the cardboard tube (as shown) and hold it in place with sticky tape or plasticine. Now test the circuit *in a darkened room* (otherwise

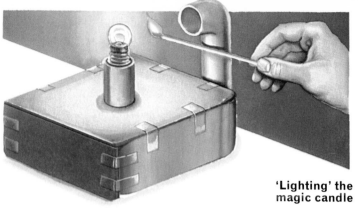

'Lighting' the
magic candle

the LDR will always be 'on'). Hold a lighted taper or match between the bulb and the LDR. The bulb should light up. To turn the candle off, hold your thumb over the LDR.

The way in which your candle works is quite simple. When no light falls on the LDR, its resistance is high and no current flows to the base leg of the transistor. This prevents a current from flowing between the collector and the emitter (that is, the transistor is switched off) and the bulb does not light up.

Light from the taper decreases the resistance of the LDR and current flows to the base leg of the transistor, which switches on and lights up the bulb. The bulb stays on when the taper is removed because its own light is falling on the LDR – until, that is, you put your thumb over the LDR.

'Blowing out'
the magic candle

When you are satisfied that your candle is working, tape the flat pieces of cardboard over the top of the holder to hide the circuitry. Now try your candle out on your friends. But this time, pretend to blow the candle out as you place your thumb over the LDR.

7: Mirrors and Lenses

Rays of light normally travel in straight lines. However, the direction in which they travel can be changed. A light ray bounces off a mirror like a ball bouncing off a wall. Also, light rays can be bent by using lenses.

Make your own periscope

A periscope uses mirrors to enable you to see over high obstacles, such as walls, and around corners. To make one you need two flat mirrors, two pieces of stiff cardboard and some balsa wood.

Mark out one piece of cardboard into four equal panels, so that when folded it will form a tall box. Score along the fold marks. Keeping the cardboard flat, cut 'windows' in the front and back panels, as shown in the drawing.

Glue strips of balsa wood to the side panels at 45° angles to the fold marks. These will support and angle the mirrors in the right direction. Fold the box into shape and insert the mirrors so that they face each other. Glue or tape the edges of

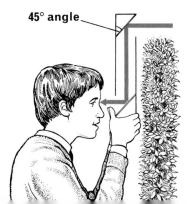

45° angle

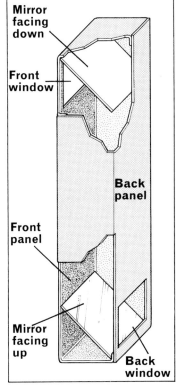

Mirror facing down

Front window

Back panel

Front panel

Mirror facing up

Back window

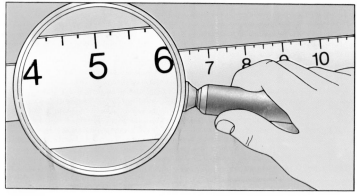

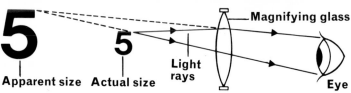

Magnifying glass

5
Apparent size

5
Actual size

Light rays

Eye

the box together. Cut two small panels from the second piece of cardboard, and tape them over the top and bottom of the periscope.

Bending light

Look at a ruler through a magnifying glass and you will find that the numbers appear larger. This is because the light rays from each number are bent by the lens so that they *appear* to come from a much larger image of the number. This is the image that is seen by the eye.

The type of lens used in a magnifying glass is called a **convex**, or converging, lens. It bends light rays toward each other. A **concave**, or diverging,

lens has the opposite effect. It makes light rays spread out.

When parallel rays of light (for example, from the Sun) are bent toward each other by a converging lens, they eventually meet and cross over. The distance between the lens and this cross-over point is called the *focal length* of the lens. A thin lens has a long focal length and a thicker, more powerful lens has a short focal length.

Making a telescope

For this you will need two lenses – a thin convex lens (focal length about 50 cm) for the *object lens* and a smaller, thicker convex lens (focal length about 5 cm) for the

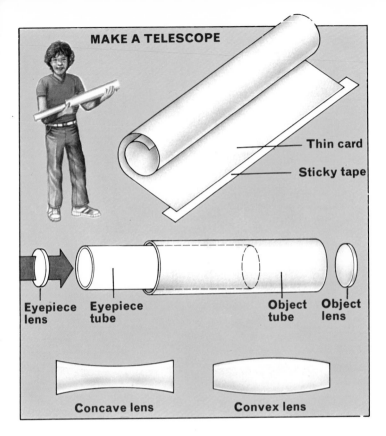

MAKE A TELESCOPE

Thin card

Sticky tape

Eyepiece lens

Eyepiece tube

Object tube

Object lens

Concave lens

Convex lens

eyepiece lens. Old spectacles are one source of lenses and an optician may help you if you explain what you are doing.

Roll a sheet of thin card into a tube so that the object lens will fit tightly into one end. Fix the tube with tape. Make a similar tube for the eyepiece lens, but make sure that this tube will slide into the object tube.

Look at an object some distance away and slide the eyepiece tube in or out until the object is in focus. DO NOT LOOK AT THE SUN THROUGH YOUR TELESCOPE, AS THIS CAN DAMAGE YOUR EYES.

With the convex eyepiece lens you will find that the image appears upside down (as with an astronomical telescope). However, if you use a concave eyepiece lens (with a short focal length), the image will appear the right way up.

41

8: Keeping Warm

Heat can move from place to place in three different ways. A glowing fire gives out heat by 'radiation'. A rising current of hot air moves by a process called 'convection'. And heat travels through a solid object by 'conduction'.

Investigating convection

THIS EXPERIMENT INVOLVES WORKING WITH A NAKED FLAME AND SHOULD BE DONE WITH GREAT CARE AND ONLY WHEN AN ADULT IS NEARBY. You will need a cardboard box (about 20 cm × 25 cm × 25 cm), a candle, some dry paper and enough cling film to cover the top of the box.

Cut off any flaps round the top of the box and make a hole in one side, as shown in the drawing above right. Dampen both the inside and the outside of the box with water. Place a piece of cling film on a table so that most of it hangs over the edge. Stand the box on its side so that the open end is above the cling film.

Now prepare a source of smoke. One method is to roll up some slightly dampened old leaves inside a piece of dry

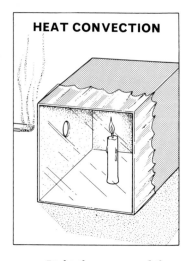

HEAT CONVECTION

paper. Light the paper and then blow out the flame so that the leaves smoulder.

Light the candle and place it carefully inside the box, near the hole. Pull the cling film up over the open front and seal it lightly to the sides. Bring your smoke source close to the hole and watch the path that the smoke takes inside the box. Within a short time it will circulate all round the box in the **convection** current produced by the heat from the candle. Warm air circulates round a room in exactly the same way as the smoke circulates round the box.

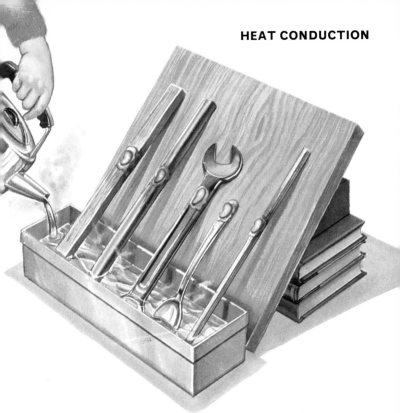

Which materials conduct heat?

If a metal teaspoon is left standing in a hot drink the handle may quickly become very hot. Heat from the liquid passes up the handle by a process called **conduction**. Different materials conduct heat at different rates.

Choose five or six objects made of different materials, which are roughly all the same size and shape. The drawing above shows a piece of wood, a copper pipe, a steel spanner, a spoon (use a silver spoon if you can) and a brass rod. Prop them up in a tin box, as shown, and stick a bean to each one, using a *very small* dab of butter. The beans should all be at the same level.

Half fill the box with boiling water and watch the beans. The one that falls off first (as the butter melts) shows you which material is the best heat **conductor.** In what order do your beans fall off?

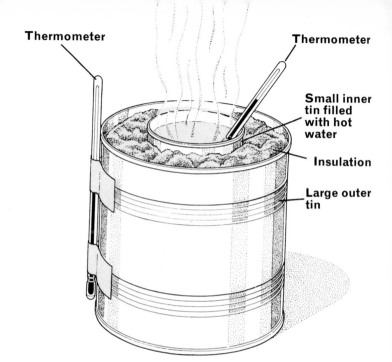

Thermometer

Thermometer

Small inner tin filled with hot water

Insulation

Large outer tin

Keeping heat in

Materials that will not allow heat to pass through them are called **insulators.** They usually work by trapping a layer of still air. This prevents the movement of heat because air is not a good conductor.

To test this, you will need two thermometers, two tin cans of different sizes and a selection of test materials, such as paper, sand, wool, water and polystyrene chips.

Put a layer of one test material in the bottom of the large can. Put the small can inside the large one and fill the space between them with more of the same material. Tape one thermometer to the outside of the large can and stand the other one in the small can.

Fill the small can with hot water and note the readings of both thermometers. Record the temperatures every five minutes for half an hour. Repeat the test with the other materials and compare the results.

Good insulators will keep the temperature of the water high for a long time (the outside temperature should remain constant). Poor insulators will let heat escape.

9: An All-Purpose Liquid

Water is vital to our lives. But because it is so plentiful (water covers nearly three quarters of the Earth's surface), its importance is often forgotten. Life as we know it on this planet would be impossible without water.

each jar or stand the printed packet or container behind it to show what it contains.

Stir the contents of the jars and leave them to settle. After about a quarter of an hour, look at each jar carefully and

What dissolves in water?

Collect together some jars and a number of different solid substances from around the kitchen. Include salt, sugar, flour, baking powder, custard powder and any others you can find.

Using a small jar as a standard measure, pour equal amounts of water into each of the larger jars. Put a level teaspoonful of a different substance into each one. Either label

estimate how much of the original solid has disappeared; that is, how much has been dissolved. How well do all the various substances dissolve?

Why do we need water?

If all the different substances that make up your body were weighed, water would be found to form the largest part – nearly two thirds of your total weight. This water is essential because

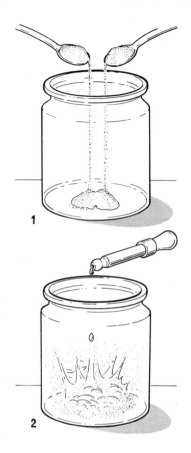

1

2

few drops of water (**2**). What happens now?

Many chemical reactions cannot occur without water. Everything that goes on in our bodies consists of a series of chemical reactions. So you can see why water is so important.

Water is also essential to us in other ways. There are many things that happen in your home, for example, that could not happen without water. Make a list of all the ones you can think of. How do you think your way of life would change if water was not easily available?

Floating and sinking

Collect together a wide variety of objects. Those shown in the drawing on the right will give you some ideas, but you should be able to find many more. Using a large bowl or basin full of water, find out which things float and which sink. Study the objects that float, and see which ride high in the water and which low. Are all the objects that float lighter than all those that sink? Do some objects float sometimes but sink if handled differently? What does a jar contain when it floats? What does it contain when it sinks?

Discovering density

The factor that controls whether or not an object sinks is the relationship between its weight

the other chemicals in your body must be dissolved in water before they can be used. Try the following experiment.

Put a level teaspoonful of bicarbonate of soda into a clean, dry jar. Then add the same quantity of powdered citric acid (from a chemist) (**1**). Mix the two together and see if anything happens. Then add a

and its *volume* (size). This factor is called the object's **density**, and it is measured by dividing the weight of the object by its volume.

The volume of an object is found by multiplying its length by its width and height. It is quite easy to work out the density of an object that has a simple shape. For example, the volume of a bar of soap that measures 8 cm long × 5 cm wide × 2 cm high is 80 cm³ (cubic centimetres). If it weighs 90 grammes, its density is $\frac{90}{80}$ = 1.1 g/cm³ (grammes per cubic centimetre).

At 4°C, fresh water has a density of 1 g/cm³. So any object with a density of more than 1 g/cm³ will sink in fresh

HYDROMETERS

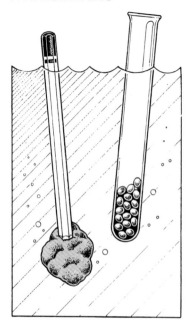

beads, lead shot fishing weights or ball bearings into a test tube. In each case you will need to adjust the weight so that the hydrometer stands upright in the water without sinking.

Put your hydrometer in the jar of fresh (unsalted) water and make a small mark on it, level with the surface of the water. Transfer it to the salty water and see how it floats. Again, mark the water level on the hydrometer to compare the density with that of fresh water. You will find that salt water (brine) is more dense than fresh water and therefore supports a floating object better.

Compare the density of warm fresh water to that of cold. You can also make up different strengths of salt water and compare them. Try testing other liquids as well, such as paraffin and methylated spirits.

water. An object having a density of less than 1 g/cm³ will float. A wooden box filled with feathers has a low density and therefore floats. The same box filled with pieces of metal has a high density and sinks.

Salt water and fresh water

Fill two jars with tap water. To one of these add two table-spoonfuls of salt. Make a **hydrometer** (a device for measuring the density of water), like the ones shown here. You can put a lump of plasticine on the end of a pencil or a straw, or you can put some

Fresh water   **Salt water**

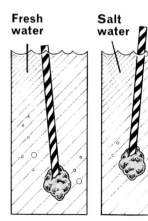

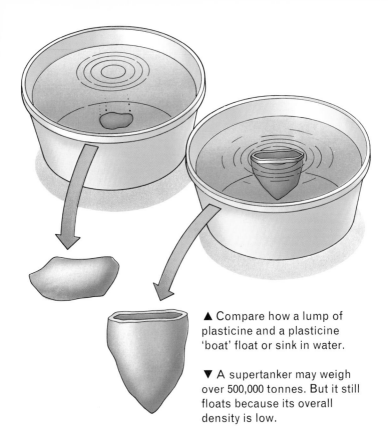

▲ Compare how a lump of plasticine and a plasticine 'boat' float or sink in water.

▼ A supertanker may weigh over 500,000 tonnes. But it still floats because its overall density is low.

49

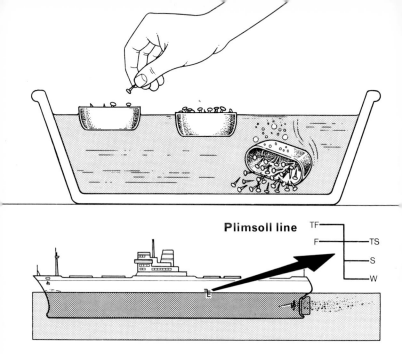

Plimsoll line

TF — F — TS — S — W

Why does a ship float?

Metal normally sinks, but many ships are made of metal and can still float. To see why this is so, try the following experiment.

Put a lump of plasticine in a bowl of water; it should sink. Now mould the plasticine into a 'boat' with fairly thin sides. Will it float this time?

By making a boat out of the plasticine you have increased its volume (size) without increasing its weight. The increase in volume consists of air (inside the boat), which has a much lower density than plasticine. So your plasticine boat has a lower density than the unshaped lump of plasticine.

How much can a boat carry?

Ships are designed to carry cargo and passengers. How much weight can your plasticine boat carry? Add small nails to your boat until it begins to sink. Then experiment with different shapes of boat, using the same piece of plasticine. What shape will carry the largest cargo without sinking?

Loading up your plasticine boat until it almost sinks shows you the maximum cargo it will hold. But the amount of cargo a

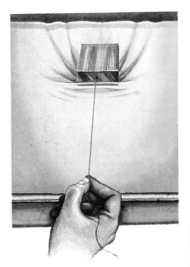

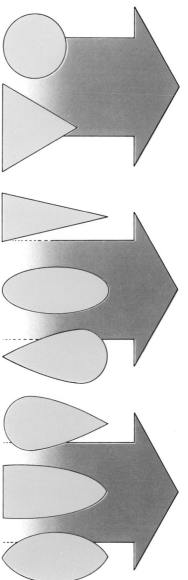

boat can carry *safely* is much less. Ships used to be overloaded and, as a result, many sank together with their crews. To prevent this happening now, every ship has a mark on the outside of its hull to show where the water level should be when it is carrying its maximum safe cargo. This mark is called the *Plimsoll Line.* Different sections of the Line apply under different conditions and in different places. **S** stands for Summer, **W** for Winter, **TS** for Tropical Summer, **F** for Fresh Water and **TF** for Tropical Fresh Water.

Finding the right shape

The shape of a boat's hull can make a great difference to its speed and use of fuel as it travels

51

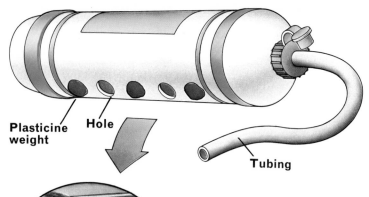

Plasticine weight **Hole** **Tubing**

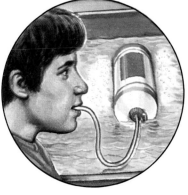

much of a wave does each one create? The best shape is the one that is easiest to pull and creates the least wave. But this will not necessarily be the one with the most pointed bow (front end).

Making a submarine

Find an old plastic washing-up liquid container and attach a piece of tubing to the nozzle. Cut some small holes in one side and stick some pieces of plasticine as weights between the holes, as shown above. You may have to hold the plasticine in place with sticky tape.

Lower your 'submarine' into the water and let it fill up and sink. Then blow down the tube until some of the water is forced out through the holes and the 'sub' begins to rise. You can alter the depth at which your submarine floats by altering the amount of air inside it.

through the water, as the following experiment will show.

Find or make a series of wooden shapes like those shown on page 51 (you may need some help with this). Screw a small hook into the front end of each shape and attach a piece of thread to it. Pull each one across a bowl or bath of water. How hard is it to pull each shape through the water? More especially, how

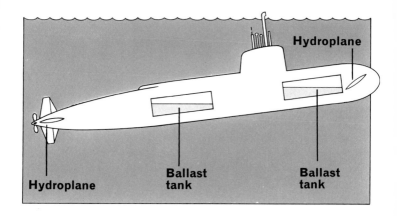

A real submarine has 'ballast tanks' that can be filled with air or water to control the depth. When the tanks are full of air the submarine comes to the surface. This is because the air in the tanks lowers the submarine's density. Submarines also have devices called 'hydroplanes', which can be adjusted to help them move upwards or downwards.

A design problem
Here is a problem for you to solve. You are allowed two sheets of paper (any size), two lollipop sticks, some sticky tape and some glue. Can you design a boat from these materials that will carry a 5p piece across a large bowl or basin filled with water? Once the boat is launched you must not actually touch it.

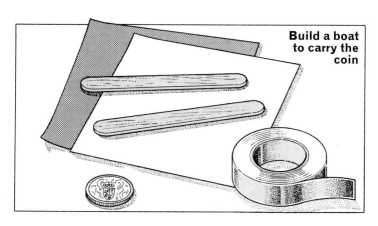

Build a boat to carry the coin

10: On the Surface

Sometimes a small object will float on water even though its density is higher than that of water. This is due to something known as 'surface tension'.

All substances are made up of small particles. These particles attract each other and it is this that holds a substance together. Below the surface of a bowl of water, each water particle is attracted equally in all directions by its neighbours. On the surface, however, the particles are attracted only downwards and sideways. The result is that the surface water particles are pulled tightly together and form a very thin 'skin' over the surface of the water. If an object is not heavy enough to force the surface particles apart, it will float on top of this 'skin', instead of sinking.

Floating a needle

Needles are made of solid metal, so it is not surprising that they normally sink in water. But a needle can be made to float. Place a needle on a small piece of newspaper, as shown below, and carefully lower the paper onto the surface of some clean water in a bowl. Avoid touching the water with your fingers.

Watch what happens. The paper will absorb the water and sink, but it does this so slowly that the surface 'skin' has time to reform between the paper and the needle. Look closely at the needle as it floats on the surface. You will see that it

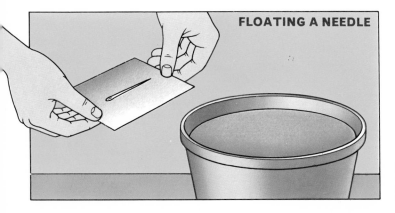

FLOATING A NEEDLE

makes a slight dent in the surface. But the **surface tension** of the water is preventing it from actually breaking through.

Altering surface tension
Leave your needle floating in the water. If it sinks, you will have to dry it carefully before you can refloat it. Put one drop of washing-up liquid into the bowl, as in the diagram on the right (don't put it too close to the needle). Watch carefully. What happens?

Detergents and soaps lower the surface tension of water by mixing with the water particles and reducing the attraction between them.

The cotton loop trick
Make a roughly circular wire loop and dip it into a bowl containing a fairly strong solution of washing-up liquid

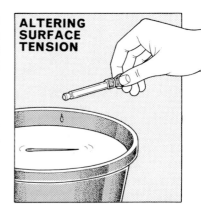

ALTERING SURFACE TENSION

and water. A film of liquid should form inside the loop (**1**). Make a small loop of cotton and place it lightly on top of the film of liquid (**2**). Make sure that it touches the film all the way round. Then, using a sharp point, break the film in the middle of the cotton loop (**3**). What happens?

You will find that the cotton loop forms a circle. Alter the shape of the wire loop and try

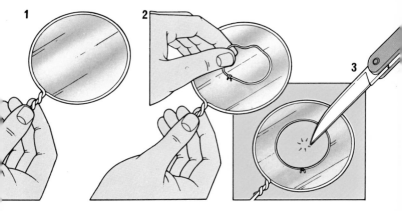

the experiment again. The result will be the same. This shows that the surface tension of the film is pulling the cotton loop equally in all directions, regardless of the shape of the wire loop.

A mothball-powered boat

Make a small boat, as shown in the drawings on the right. Shape the hull from a sheet of thick balsa wood (about 15 cm × 6 cm × 1 cm). Wash out a large bowl thoroughly, making sure that it does not contain any trace of grease, soap or detergent. Fill the bowl with clean water and leave it to settle.

Wedge a piece of mothball (camphor) into the notch at the back of the boat and carefully lower the boat into the water, making as little disturbance as possible. Let go of the boat and you will find that it slowly moves away from you across the bowl. The camphor lowers the surface tension of the water behind the boat. As a result, the surface tension of the water in front of the boat pulls it along.

Insects and surface tension

Several kinds of insect, such as the pond skaters shown in the photograph on the right, make use of surface tension to keep them above water. Some others, like the larvae of gnats and mosquitoes, hang onto the surface film from underneath.

In some tropical countries, mosquitoes spread the disease malaria. One method of controlling this problem is to spray the swamps in which the mosquitoes breed with detergent. This reduces the surface tension of the water and prevents the larvae from hanging onto the surface. They sink to the bottom and die before they can mature into adult mosquitoes.

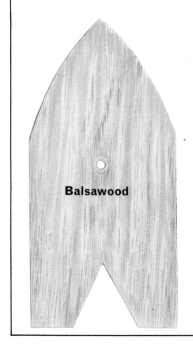

A MOTHBALL BOAT

Balsawood

▶ Pond skaters standing on the water surface. The surface tension of the water forms a skin which prevents the insects from sinking.

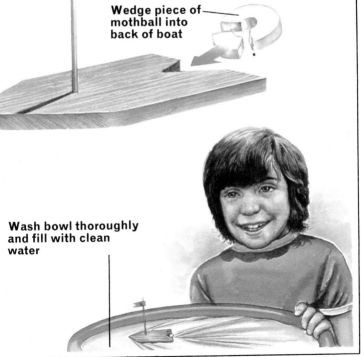

Wedge piece of mothball into back of boat

Wash bowl thoroughly and fill with clean water

11: What is Soil?

Soil is vital to life on Earth. The Sun's energy can be taken in and used only by green plants. Soil provides the plants with a firm anchorage, and supplies them with water and minerals. Without soil there would be no plants, and so no animals.

Soil is more than just mud or dirt. If you look at a lump of soil carefully, you will see that it contains many different things.

▲ A soil 'profile' shows that the ground beneath us is made up of several layers. Below the topsoil lie one or more layers of subsoil, which rests on solid rock.

In fact, soil is a mixture of six main components. These are **humus** (dead plant and animal material), rock particles, water, **minerals**, air and living things.

How much water does soil contain?

To do this experiment you will have to ask if you can use the kitchen scales. The only other thing you will need is a tin foil or metal pie dish. The weight of an empty foil dish will not register on most ordinary kitchen scales. But if you use a metal pie dish, weigh it as accurately as possible (1) and write down the weight.

Fill the dish with at least 200 grammes of fresh soil. Weigh it again (2) and write down the weight. Leave the dish in a dry place for several days so that the water in the soil can evaporate. Then weigh the dish and soil again (3).

The proportion of water in your soil sample can be calculated from the figures you have written down. Here is an example of a typical calculation:

Weight of dish = 40 grammes.
Weight of dish and wet soil = 250 grammes.
Therefore, weight of wet soil sample = 250 − 40 = 210 grammes.
After drying, weight of dish and dry soil = 180 grammes.
Therefore, weight of water in soil = 250 − 180 = 70 grammes.

The percentage of water in the soil is found by dividing the

WEIGHING THE WATER IN SOIL

1

2

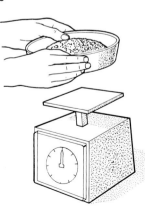

3

FINDING THE AMOUNT OF HUMUS IN SOIL

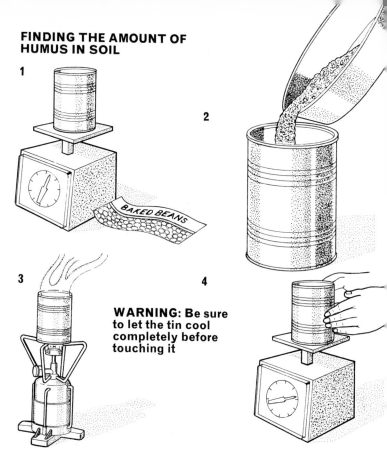

1

2

3

4

WARNING: Be sure to let the tin cool completely before touching it

BAKED BEANS

weight of the water (70 grammes) by the weight of the wet soil (210 grammes) and multiplying the result by 100. The answer in this case is 33%.

Will soil burn?

Weigh an empty tin can (**1**) and write down the weight. Carefully tip the dry soil from the last experiment into the can (**2**), making sure that you do not

spill any, and weigh the can again. Heat the can of soil on a camping stove for about 20 minutes (**3**). It is best to do this outside, or in a garage, as it makes a rather unpleasant smell. TAKE CARE TO KEEP THE FLAME AWAY FROM ANYTHING THAT COULD CATCH FIRE. Allow the can to COOL COMPLETELY before weighing it again (**4**); a hot can may damage the scales as well as burning your fingers!

Your soil sample will have lost weight. This is because the humus has been burnt away. By subtracting the weight of the burned soil from the original weight of the unburned, dry soil you can find the weight of the humus. To find the percentage, divide the weight of humus by the weight of the unburned soil and multiply the result by 100.

Separating the soil 'skeleton'

You have now removed the water and the humus from your soil sample, but you still have the mixture of rock particles. This is known as the **mineral skeleton.** To find the weight of the mineral skeleton in your sample, subtract the weight of the tin can from the total weight of the burned soil and the can. The percentage of rock particles in your soil is then found by dividing the weight of the mineral skeleton by the weight of the unburned soil, and by multiplying the answer by 100.

The mineral skeleton is made up of many variously sized particles. Put about 5-cm depth of your soil sample into a tall jar and fill the jar three-quarters full with clean water. Put a top on the jar and shake it vigorously to mix the soil with the water. Watch the soil settle into different layers. Carefully measure the depth of each layer to find the proportions of the

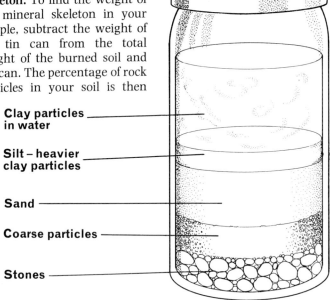

Clay particles in water

Silt – heavier clay particles

Sand

Coarse particles

Stones

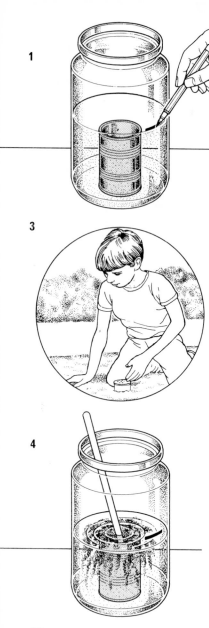

1

2

3

4

MEASURING THE AMOUNT OF AIR IN SOIL

particle types. You can draw and label the layers as shown on page 61.

Measuring the air in soil

Fill up a tin can with water and then tip the water into a measuring jug. Write down the amount of water you have. This gives you a measure of the volume of the tin can.

Next, place the empty can in a large jar half filled with water and mark the water level on the outside of the jar (**1**). Remove a canful of water (**2**) and pour it away.

Punch a few holes in the bottom of the can and push it, open end down, into some fresh

soil (3). Dig the can out, level off the soil with the top of the can and place the can and the soil in the jar.

At first, the water level will rise to the water mark. But as air is released from the soil it will gradually fall. You can help this process by stirring up the soil (4). Now add water from the measuring jug until the water level is again up to the mark. The volume of water you add is equal to the volume of air that was released from the soil. To find the percentage of air, divide the volume of air by the volume of soil (that is, the volume of the tin can) and multiply by 100.

▲ Using a soil test kit to find the pH of soil. The kit will also indicate how much lime should be added to an acid soil.

Is your garden acid or alkaline?

You can find the pH value (see page 6) of your garden soil by using a simple soil test kit. Follow the instructions in your kit carefully. The pH of your soil is important because most plants grow best within a small range of pH values. Adding manure or lime alters the pH of soil, and so the pH of a vegetable garden, for example, can change over a period of time. To get healthy plants it may be

PLANTING MAIZE SEEDS

necessary to correct the pH of the soil occasionally.

Why use fertilizers?

If your soil is poor and lacks the proper minerals, it may be improved by adding a fertilizer. Try the following experiment.

Plant some maize seeds in a seed tray, as shown above. When the seedlings have a few leaves, transfer six of them to jars or bottles, as shown on the opposite page, containing: soil (1); soil and five drops of liquid fertilizer (2); tap water (3); distilled water – you can use melted ice from the sides of your fridge or freezer (4); tap water and five drops of fertilizer (5); distilled water and five drops of fertilizer (6). Put straws in the bottles and use cotton wool to support the seedlings and the straws.

Leave the seedlings for about ten days. Keep the soil jars

moist with tap water, and blow gently through the straws every day for about half a minute to keep the water in the bottles supplied with oxygen. Which of your seedlings grow best?

Comparing soils

Get some samples of soil from several different places. If possible, include chalky, sandy and clay soils. You will need enough of each soil to do all the tests indicated on the 'Growth Chart' below, and fill a seed tray. Repeat the soil tests for each type of soil, then copy out the chart below and fill in your results.

For the 'Growth' results, fill each seed tray two-thirds full of a different type of soil and sprinkle them with some mixed poultry corn (from a pet shop)..

	Acid or Alkaline	Amount of Air
Soil A	Slightly acid	30%
Soil B		
Soil C		

Cover the seeds with another centimetre or so of the soil and lightly press down the surface with a piece of wood. Moisten each tray with water, but do not swamp it.

Cover the trays with sheets of glass or cling film, until the seeds start to show above the surface. Keep the soil moist and see how well the plants grow over a period of about ten days. Which type of soil produces the best growth? Fill in the growth results on your chart. Now look at the results of the other soil tests and see if you can decide which soil factors have had the

GROWTH CHART							
Amount of Water	Amount of Humus	Proportions in burned Soil of			Growth of Seedlings		
		Clay	Sand	Stones	Good	Fair	Poor
8%	10%	4 parts	3 parts	3 parts	✓		

greatest influence on the growth of your 'crops'.

What minerals must soil have?
This experiment will show you what happens to plants when certain minerals are missing from the soil. You will need nine 2-litre (about 4 pints) plastic bottles, nine smaller jars, some thick black paper, straws, cotton wool and the chemicals shown on the chart opposite. You should be able to get these chemicals from garden shops or chemists. Major toy shops should also have them. You will also need some of the seedlings that you grew for the last experiment.

Cut circles out of the paper, large enough to cover the tops of the small jars. Cut in to the centre from one edge and cut a hole in the middle of each circle for the plant stem (as shown on page 74). Make another small hole near the edge of each circle for a straw. Cover the sides of the jars with black paper.

Make up the nine solutions with water, according to the instructions on the chart. Put one solution in each of the plastic bottles and label them with the number of the solution. Fill each small jar with a solution and label these also. Keep the remainder in the plastic bottles in a dark place.

		MINERALS
4 pts Water	1 teaspoon	¼ teaspoon
1	Potassium nitrate	Magnesium sulphate
2	Potassium sulphate	Magnesium sulphate
3	Calcium nitrate	Magnesium sulphate
4	Potassium nitrate	
5	Potassium nitrate	Magnesium nitrate
6	Potassium nitrate	Magnesium sulphate
7	Potassium nitrate	Magnesium sulphate
8	Potassium nitrate	Magnesium sulphate
9	Small quantity of soil in water	

NECESSARY FOR GROWTH

¼ teaspoon	¼ teaspoon	Minerals present in solution	Minerals missing
Iron phosphate	Calcium sulphate	Potassium, Nitrogen, Magnesium, Sulphur, Iron, Phosphorus, Calcium	None
Iron phosphate	Calcium sulphate	Potassium, Magnesium, Sulphur, Iron, Phosphorus, Calcium	Nitrogen
Iron phosphate	Calcium sulphate	Nitrogen, Magnesium, Sulphur, Iron, Phosphorus, Calcium	Potassium
Iron phosphate	Calcium sulphate	Potassium, Nitrogen, Iron, Phosphorus, Calcium, Sulphur	Magnesium
Iron phosphate	Calcium nitrate	Potassium, Nitrogen, Magnesium, Iron, Phosphorus, Calcium	Sulphur
Iron sulphate	Calcium sulphate	Potassium, Nitrogen, Magnesium, Iron, Calcium, Sulphur	Phosphorus
Sodium phosphate	Calcium sulphate	Potassium, Nitrogen, Magnesium, Sulphur, Phosphorus, Calcium, (Sodium)	Iron
Iron phosphate		Potassium, Nitrogen, Magnesium, Sulphur, Iron, Phosphorus	Calcium
		All those in solution 1, plus other trace elements	None

BUILDING A WORMERY

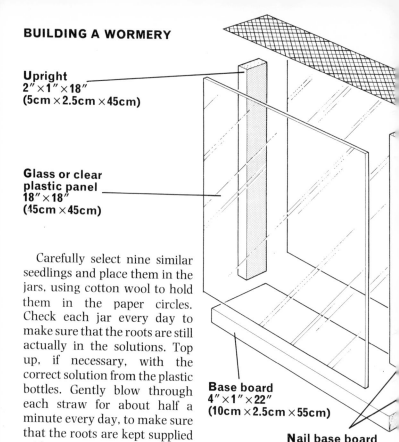

Upright
2″×1″×18″
(5cm ×2.5cm ×45cm)

Glass or clear plastic panel
18″×18″
(45cm ×45cm)

Base board
4″×1″×22″
(10cm ×2.5cm ×55cm)

Nail base board to upright

Carefully select nine similar seedlings and place them in the jars, using cotton wool to hold them in the paper circles. Check each jar every day to make sure that the roots are still actually in the solutions. Top up, if necessary, with the correct solution from the plastic bottles. Gently blow through each straw for about half a minute every day, to make sure that the roots are kept supplied with oxygen.

Look for any changes that occur over a period of three weeks, keeping notes and draw-ings of the changes that you see. Which minerals do you think are most important?

Living things in the soil

Vast numbers of small plants and animals live in the soil. They help to make humus by breaking down dead plant and animal material. In this way, they help to improve the mineral content of the soil.

Of all the soil animals, earthworms are probably the most easily observed. You can study earthworms by building a wormery, as shown in the drawing. Ask an adult to help you cut the wood to size and nail through the bottom board

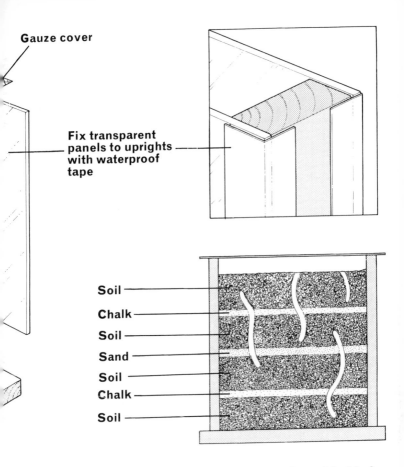

Gauze cover

Fix transparent panels to uprights with waterproof tape

Soil
Chalk
Soil
Sand
Soil
Chalk
Soil

into the two uprights. Attach the glass or plastic sides with waterproof tape.

Put about 10-cm depth of soil into the wormery and then add a layer of chalk about $\frac{1}{2}$-cm deep. Build up the layers of soil, chalk or sand as shown, and place three or four worms on top. Cover the wormery with a piece of gauze and enclose the transparent sides with black paper. Look each day to see what your worms have been doing.

After a few days, try putting small quantities of different foods, such as dead leaves, grated carrot, grass and apple peel on top of the soil. Do worms prefer certain foods? What do they do with their food?

12: Looking at Plants

Plants collect energy from the Sun and use it to make food. They also collect water and minerals from the soil. The roots, the stems and the leaves of plants all have a different part to play in these important activities.

The energy collectors of plants are their leaves. These vary considerably in size, shape, thickness and colour. The drawings below show a few examples. See how many different types you can find, and draw their shapes.

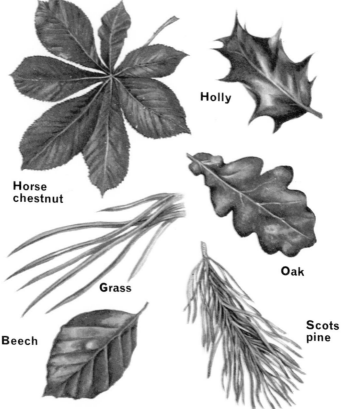

Holly

Horse chestnut

Grass

Beech

Oak

Scots pine

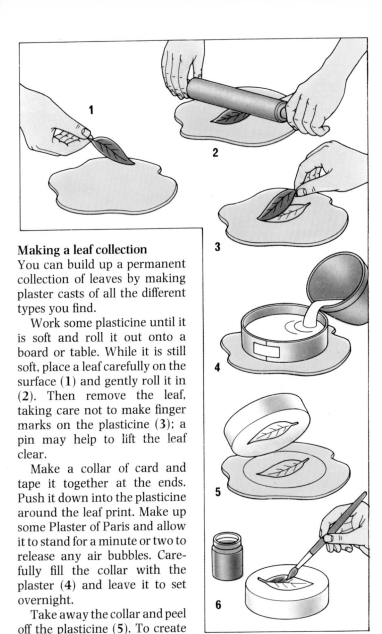

Making a leaf collection

You can build up a permanent collection of leaves by making plaster casts of all the different types you find.

Work some plasticine until it is soft and roll it out onto a board or table. While it is still soft, place a leaf carefully on the surface (**1**) and gently roll it in (**2**). Then remove the leaf, taking care not to make finger marks on the plasticine (**3**); a pin may help to lift the leaf clear.

Make a collar of card and tape it together at the ends. Push it down into the plasticine around the leaf print. Make up some Plaster of Paris and allow it to stand for a minute or two to release any air bubbles. Carefully fill the collar with the plaster (**4**) and leave it to set overnight.

Take away the collar and peel off the plasticine (**5**). To create

Tomato

Apple

Plum

Dandelion

the best effect, you should paint your leaf cast (6) and then varnish it, after the paint has dried, to protect it.

Fruits and seeds

Many plants produce fruits which contain seeds. The seeds have to be scattered before they can grow and different plants have different methods for doing this. Most berries and soft fruits are eaten and carried away by animals. The seeds then pass through unharmed. Other fruits have hooks that catch in animals' fur as they brush past. A number of fruits explode, throwing out the seeds. Make a collection of fruits in the autumn and see if you can decide how each type of seed is dispersed.

Some fruits have special structures that allow them to be carried by the wind. Dandelion fruits, for example, have parachute-like plumes. Some trees, such as sycamore and ash, have winged fruits. See if you can find other fruits with parachutes or wings.

How far can seeds fly?

For this experiment you will need to borrow a hair drier. You

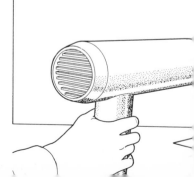

Drop seeds, one at a time, down tube into air stream

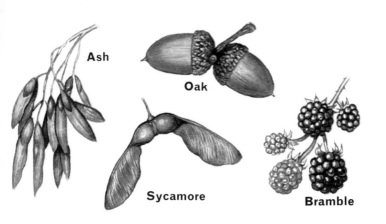

Ash

Oak

Sycamore

Bramble

will also need a large sheet of paper (about a metre long), a tube and a wooden block.

Collect a variety of seeds and fruits, including as many as possible with wings or parachutes. Arrange the block and paper as shown in the drawing below, and get a friend to hold the tube for you.

Hold the drier close to the bottom of the tube and switch it on to full speed. TAKE CARE NOT TO LET ANY OF THE SEEDS GET SUCKED INTO THE BACK OF THE DRYER. Drop the seeds down the tube one at a time and watch how they fly through the air. Mark where they land on the paper, using a different colour for each different type of seed.

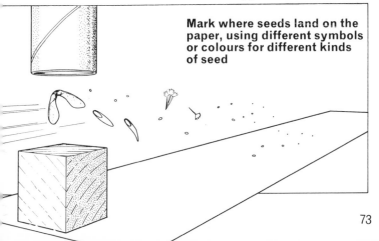

Mark where seeds land on the paper, using different symbols or colours for different kinds of seed

Cotton wool

Cardboard lid with hole cut in centre to support stem

Water with ink

What do plant stems do?

The stem of a plant holds the leaves up in the air so that they can make the best possible use of the sunlight. It also carries vital water and minerals from the roots up to the leaves. And it carries energy-giving food down to the roots.

You can do a simple experiment to investigate how water travels up a stem. Put some coloured ink into a jar three-quarters full of water. Cut out a paper or cardboard lid for the jar and fit a young plant into the lid as shown above. Lower the plant into the ink and leave it for about half an hour.

Remove the plant from the jar and cut it across the stem. Look carefully at the cut end, using a magnifying glass if possible.

You will see that only some areas of the stem are stained

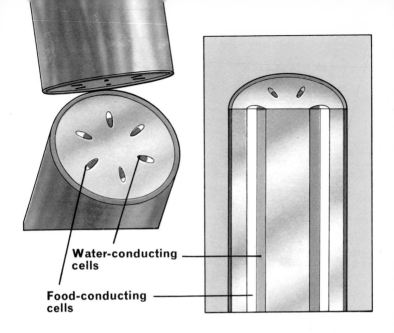

Water-conducting cells

Food-conducting cells

with ink. These areas contain the cells that carry water up the stem. Now cut the stem along its length and you should see the stained areas running all the way up the stem, as shown in the picture above.

You can also use this experiment to find out how fast water travels up a stem. Without using the cardboard top, put several similar plants into the jar of ink and take one plant out every two minutes. Keep a note of the length of time each plant was in the water.

Remove the leaves immediately and, starting from the top, cut off short lengths of the stem until you find the upper limit of the ink. When you have done this to all the plants, measure the distance from the roots to the top of the ink in each case.

Now divide the length of each stem (root to top of ink) by the time it was in the water. For example, if you have a piece of stem 8 cm long from a plant that you took out of the ink after 4 minutes, then the speed at which the ink (water) travelled up the stem was $\frac{8}{4} = 2$ cm per minute. Compare the results for each stem.

Try this experiment on a windy day, a hot day, a cold day and a wet day and see if the results are different.

Glossary

Acid A sour substance that has a pH value of between 1 and 6. Strong acids can be very harmful.

Alkali A substance that has a pH value of between 8 and 14. An alkali can be used to neutralize an acid.

Carbohydrate An energy-containing chemical made up of carbon, hydrogen and oxygen. Examples include sugar and starch.

Chromatography A method of separating certain chemicals by allowing a liquid containing the chemicals to move through an absorbent material.

Circuit, electrical The path taken by an electric current.

Concave lens A lens in which the surfaces are curved inwards. The lens is therefore thinner at the middle than at the edges. A concave lens causes rays of light to diverge (spread out).

Conduction The movement of heat or electricity through a material.

Conductor A material that allows the movement of heat or electricity by conduction.

Convection The movement of heat through a gas, such as air, or a liquid, by means of the movement of the gas or liquid itself.

Convex lens A lens in which the surfaces are curved outwards. The lens is therefore thicker at the middle than at the edges. A convex lens converges (brings together) rays of light.

Density The property of a material that is defined by its mass (weight) per unit of volume (size). It is usually expressed as grammes per cubic centimetre (g/cm^3).

Digestion The physical and chemical breakdown of food.

Electromagnet A temporary magnet, made from an iron core surrounded by a coil of wire carrying an electric current.

Electroplating Coating a material with a metal, such as copper, tin, nickel or chromium, by using an electric current.

Enzyme A special protein that speeds up the rate of a chemical reaction in a living plant or animal. Many enzymes are important in digestion.

Fat An energy-containing chemical made up of carbon,

hydrogen and oxygen, but in different proportions to those of a carbohydrate.

Humus The dead remains of plants and animals in the soil.

Hydrometer An instrument for determining the density of a liquid.

Indicator A dye that will change colour when mixed with other chemicals to show differences between certain chemicals, or to show the end of a chemical reaction.

Insulator A material that prevents the conduction of heat or electricity.

Light dependent resistor (LDR) A variable resistor which is affected by light intensity. The resistance decreases as the light gets brighter.

Minerals Elements, such as iron, potassium and calcium, which are needed for healthy growth and are found in soil and in food.

Mineral skeleton Rock particles of varying size that form the major part of soil.

Neutral Neither acid nor alkaline. Has a pH value of 7.

pH value A numerical value given to the acidity or alkalinity of a chemical.

Power The *rate* of doing work, calculated by dividing the work done by the time taken to do it.

Protein A complicated chemical made up of carbon, hydrogen, oxygen and nitrogen. Proteins are used to build and repair living cells.

Radiation The movement of heat, light and other forms of energy (e.g. X-rays and radio waves) in wave-like rays that travel in straight lines.

Resistor An electrical or electronic component that restricts the flow of an electric current in a circuit.

Solution A mixture of a solid and a liquid (usually water) in which the particles that make up the solid are fully dispersed among the particles of the liquid.

Surface tension The tension in the surface film of a liquid caused by the attraction of the liquid particles to each other.

Titration A chemical method of finding the strength of one solution by allowing it to react with a measured amount of another solution.

Transistor An electronic device that can be used to amplify (increase) the current flowing in a circuit, or to switch a current on and off.

Work Any task or function that uses energy. *Work done* is calculated by multiplying the force used by the distance moved.

Index

Page numbers in *italics* refer to illustrations.

A

Acids 6–11, 76; household 6–11, *7*, 46; in soil 63, *63*; sulphuric 6, 29; titration 10–11, *10*, 77
Air: convection 42, *42*, 76; in soil 58, 62–63, *62*; insulation 44, *44*
Alcohol 16
Alkalis 6–11, 76; household 6–11, *7*; in soil 63, *63*; titration 10–11, *10*, 77
Animals 20, 58, 68

B

Ballast tank 53, *53*
Base leg 35, *35*, *37*, 38
Battery 24, *24*, 25, *25*, 27, *27*, *28*, 29, *29*, *30*, 31, 32, *32*, *33*, 34, 35, 36, *36*, 37, *37*; car 6, 29
Bell, electric 31–33, *32*, *33*
Bread making 16–17, *17*
Breathing rate, 22, *22*
Bulb, light 24, *24*, 25, *25*, 26, *26*, 27, *27*, 28, 29, *29*, 30, 34, 35, 36, *36*, 37, *37*, 38, *38*; holder 24, *24*, 25, *25*, *26*, 27, *27*, 29, *29*, 30, 34, *37*

C

Cables, high voltage *23*
Calcium *67*
Candle, electronic 34–38, *36–38*
Carbohydrates 12, *12*, 14, 76
Carbon dioxide gas 16
Chemicals 4, 6–19, *6–19*, 46
Chromatography 18–19, *18–19*, 76

Circuit, electrical 24–26, *24*, *25*, 34, 35, 36, 76; diagram 35–36, *36*; short 26
Coil 31
Collector leg 35, *35*, *37*, 38
Colour chart (pH) 6, 8, *8–9*
Concave lens 40, 41, *41*, 76
Conduction 42, 43, *43*, 76
Conductor 43, *43*, 44, 76
Convection 42, *42*, 76
Convex lens 40, 41, *41*, 76
Copper sulphate 28, *28*, 29

D

Density 46, 47, *47*, 48, *48*, 49, 50, 53, 54, 76
Digestion 13, 15, 76
Dropper, eye *7*, 10, *10*, 11, *11*, 12
Dyes 18, 19

E

Earthworm 68, 69, *69*
Electric bell 31–33, *32*, *33*
Electricity 23–38, *23–38*
Electromagnet *30*, 31–33, *32*, *33*, 76
Electronics 34–38, *34–38*
Electroplating 28, *28*, 76
Emitter leg 35, *35*, *37*, 38
End point 10, 11
Energy: chemical 12, 14; electrical 23–38, *23–38*; heat 23; solar *20*, 58, 70, 74
Enzymes 13, 14, 15, 76

F

Fats 12, 14, *14*, 76–77
Fertilizer 64
Floating 46, 47, *47*, 48, *48*, 49, 50, *50*, 54, *54*, 55, *55*

Focal length 40
Food chemistry 6–17, *6–17*, 20, 23
Force 20, 21
Fruits 72–73, *72–73*
Fuse, electric 25, *25*

G

Gas: carbon dioxide 16
Generator, electric 31
Gravity 20, 21
Grease spot test 14, *14*
Growth chart, plant 64–66, *64–65*

H

Heat 42–44, *42–44*
Horsepower 21
Hulls (ships) 51–52, *50*
Humus 58, *60*, 61, 68, 77
Hydrometer 48, *48*, 77
Hydroplane 53, *53*

I

Indicator 6–11, *8*, 77; homemade 8–10, *9*; Universal 6, *8–9*, 11
Ink experiments 18–19, *18–19*
Insects, on water surface 56, 57, *57*
Insulation 25, 44, *44*
Insulator 44, 77
Iodine 12, 13, *13*, 14
Iron *67*

J

Joules 21

K

Kitchen chemicals 6–11, *6–11*

L

LDR *see* Light dependent resistor
Leaves 70, *70*, 71–72, *71*, 74, *74*
Legs, transistor 35, *35*